Sarah, Plain and Tall

by Patricia MacLachlan

Danielle Denega

SCHOLASTIC REFERENCE

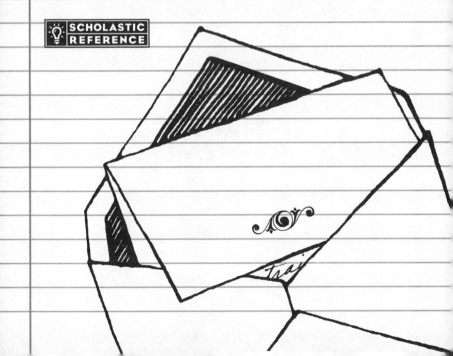

Library of Congress Cataloging-in-Publication Data

Scholastic BookFiles: A Reading Guide to Sarah, Plain and Tall by Patricia MacLachlan/Danielle Denega.   p. cm.

Summary: Discusses the writing, characters, plot, and themes of this 1986 Newbery Award–winning book. Includes discussion questions and activities. Includes bibliographical references (p.).

1. MacLachlan, Patricia. Sarah, Plain and Tall—Juvenile literature.
2. Frontier and pioneer life in literature—Juvenile literature.
[1. MacLachlan, Patricia. Sarah, Plain and Tall.   2. American literature—History and criticism.]   I. Title.   II. Series.

PS3563.A3178S373   2004

813′.54—dc21   2003042573

0-439-29798-2

10 9 8 7 6 5 4 3 2 1   04 05 06 07 08

Composition by Brad Walrod/High Text Graphics, Inc.
Cover and interior design by Red Herring Design

Printed in the U.S.A.   23
First printing, March 2004

Contents

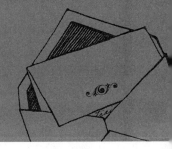

About Patricia MacLachlan

"There is no better model than a good book."

—Patricia MacLachlan

When Patricia MacLachlan talks about her career as a writer, she says that she always knew she wanted to write. But when she was young she thought that it was a job that she couldn't do. MacLachlan explains, "First, let me say that as a child I made a conscious decision not to be a writer because I thought writers had all the answers." MacLachlan eventually came to understand that people write to help *find* answers to their questions and to help them understand life better. As an adult she finally got up the courage to try it. Although she had a late start, she went on to become an award-winning author.

Patricia Pritzkau (MacLachlan) was born on March 3, 1938, in Cheyenne, Wyoming, and was raised in Minnesota. Both states are in the western part of the United States. MacLachlan says that even though she moved east as an adult, she never let go of the bond she formed with her roots: "I have an amazingly close connection to the prairie. Each time I return I feel like I am home." It was this relationship with the West that helped her create the vivid setting in *Sarah, Plain and Tall*: "Sarah came in the spring. She came through green grass fields that bloomed with Indian paintbrush, red and orange, and blue-eyed grass. . . . Gophers ran back and forth across the road, stopping to stand up and watch the wagon. Far off in the field a woodchuck ate and listened. Ate and listened."

MacLachlan has no brothers or sisters, but did have a very close relationship with her parents throughout her childhood. She spent much of her time with her dad, Philo, and her mom, Madonna, so their influences molded her as a person. Her parents were both schoolteachers and brought many books into their household. They encouraged her to "read a book and find out who you are," so she became an avid reader. She had an extremely active imagination and would often read a book and then act out scenes from it with her father.

Patricia eventually moved to the East Coast. In 1962, she graduated from the University of Connecticut and married psychologist Robert MacLachlan. Like her parents, she became a teacher. She taught English at Bennett Junior High School in Manchester, Connecticut, from 1963 until 1979.

The MacLachlans have three children: John, Jamie, and Emily. Patricia spent a great deal of time reading to her kids when they were young, just as her parents had done with her when she was a child. Her family has always been a very important part of her life. But as her kids grew older and became more independent, she began to feel "a need to do something else."

At the age of thirty-five MacLachlan, in addition to teaching, was working at the Children's Aid Family Service Agency. She interviewed possible foster mothers and wrote articles about adoption and foster care. It was at this time that she realized her concern for families and children and her commitment to children's literature were what really excited her. MacLachlan decided she wanted to pursue writing for kids. She says, "It dawned on me that what I really wanted to do was to write. How would I ever have the courage, I wondered. It was very scary to find myself in the role of student again, trying to learn something new."

With the full support of her family, MacLachlan decided to give herself a few years to become a published author. If the time passed and she was unsuccessful, she would give up and try a different profession. But she did get published, and in only one year! Her first book, *The Sick Day*, was released in 1979. It is a picture book about a little girl with a cold, whose father cares for her. One of the people who believed in MacLachlan's abilities as a writer early on was an editor (a person whose job it is to help authors develop their writing skills) named Charlotte Zolotow. She said that MacLachlan's writing is good because it is "filled with beautiful images, a poetic voice, and sensitive insights strung together like free verse."

MacLachlan's stories are usually about families. She has said that many of them, like *Sarah, Plain and Tall*; *The Facts and Fictions of Minna Pratt*; and *Cassie Binegar*, are partly autobiographical (a story about a person's life that is written by the person herself). MacLachlan describes them this way:

"My books derive chiefly from my family life, both as a child with my own parents as well as with my husband and kids." *The Sick Day* was followed, very quickly, by many popular and successful titles, including *Sarah, Plain and Tall*. Since then her books have won countless awards, including the Newbery Medal and the Christopher Award, which are two of the most distinguished awards a children's writer can receive.

MacLachlan attributes her success to her family, for inspiring the themes she writes about and for being completely behind her when she chose to switch careers and become a writer. She says, "They have always supported the process as well as the end results."

Writers don't always have a regular paycheck coming to them, like people with other jobs, so this meant that while she was first starting out, MacLachlan's family would have only her husband's salary on which to live. He told Patricia, "What you're doing is more important than money." MacLachlan feels strongly that she would not have become the successful writer she is today if her husband had not given her time and space to develop her craft. She says, "...no one supported me more than my husband, Bob, who during the early single-salary years wouldn't let me stop writing for a 'real' job."

The MacLachlans now live in Massachusetts, where they spend part of the time at their house in Leeds and the rest of the time at their house on Cape Cod. Patricia continues to write, give lectures, and teach a course on children's literature at Smith College.

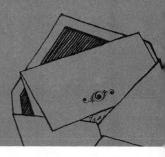

How *Sarah, Plain and Tall* Came About

"Writing Sarah was in a sense, like a going back home."

—Patricia MacLachlan

In 1985, just six years after publishing her very first book, *Sarah, Plain and Tall* was released. The book received praise from children, parents, teachers, and literary critics alike. One critic even called *Sarah, Plain and Tall* "a near perfect miniature novel."

In 1986, *Sarah, Plain and Tall* won the John Newbery Medal from the American Library Association. The award is represented by the gold seal you may see on the book's cover. Every year, this honor is given to the author of the most distinguished piece of children's literature from the previous year. In her acceptance speech for the award, MacLachlan told the audience that it was her mother who inspired her to write this heartwarming story.

Patricia explained that when she was a child, her mother told her about a woman she knew who had moved from the coast of Maine to the prairie. This woman became a wife and mother to some family members of Patricia's mother. Yet it wasn't until her own children were preparing to go away to college that Patricia made the connection between the story her mother had shared with her and her own memories of life on the prairie.

Before Patricia's children left for college, her parents took the MacLachlans on a trip to the prairie, where she and her parents had been born. MacLachlan spoke about this trip in her Newbery acceptance speech: "It was a gift for all of us, for the children to see a land they had never seen, to know family they had never met, to stand on the vast North Dakota farm where my father had been born in a sod house." The family trip to see her birthplace brought back many memories for her and her parents.

Memories were especially important for MacLachlan because her mother had developed Alzheimer's disease. Alzheimer's disease is a serious illness that causes a person to gradually lose her memory. Patricia told the Newbery audience, "Sarah speaks for me and my mother, for whom there are few words left. . . ."

MacLachlan says the desire to preserve the memories of her mother, and to tell the story of their family and of the prairie itself, propelled her to write *Sarah, Plain and Tall*: "When I began *Sarah*, I wished for several things and was granted something unexpected. Most of all I wished to write my mother's story with spaces, like the prairie, with silences that could say what words could not. . . . And in the end we are all there, my mother, my father, my husband, my children, and me."

Chapter Charter:
Questions to Guide Your Reading

The following questions will help you think about the important parts of each chapter.

Chapter 1
- Why do you think Caleb asks Anna about their mother so often?
- When Caleb asks his father why he does not sing anymore, his father replies, "I've forgotten the old songs." Do you think there's another reason why he may not sing anymore? What might it be?
- In her very first letter to Jacob, Sarah tells him that she is not mild mannered. Why might she feel it is important to tell him this?
- Why do you think it is important to Anna that her father ask Sarah if she sings?

Chapter 2
- What does Sarah tell the children about Maine in her letters? Why do you think she includes these details?
- Why do you think Caleb reads Sarah's letter so many times?
- When Anna sets the table, she sets four places and then puts one away. Whom do you think the fourth setting was meant for? Why does she put it away?

Chapter 3

- Why does Papa get dressed up for Sarah's arrival? Why do you think Caleb asks Anna so many questions while they are waiting for Sarah and Papa to return?
- Why does Sarah bring Caleb and Anna gifts from the sea?
- Anna says, "I wished we had a sea of our own." What do you think she means? Why would she wish for this?

Chapter 4

- When Sarah listens to the conch shell, Anna notices that Sarah looks sad. Have you ever felt sad about missing a person or a place?
- Caleb keeps noticing things that Sarah says, and he tells Anna, "That means Sarah will stay." Do you think Caleb wants Sarah to stay or leave? What parts of the story support your opinion?
- When they sing a song with Sarah, Papa "sang as if he had never stopped singing." What do you think that means about the way Papa is feeling?

Chapter 5

- When the lamb is found dead, Sarah cries and will not let the children near it. What do you think this says about her personality?
- Why do you think Papa makes the hay dune for Sarah?
- After Papa builds the hay dune, Caleb asks Sarah if she is scared to climb it. Sarah is not scared at all. Have you ever been brave when other people were afraid?
- How do you think Papa feels about Sarah?

Chapter 6

- Sarah asks the children about winter even though it is still spring. Why do you think she wonders about winter?
- How does the author describe summer and winter on the prairie, and the ocean in Maine? What types of words does she use? Can you imagine what these places might be like based on her words?
- After they all go for a swim in the cow pond, Anna dozes off and dreams a "perfect" dream? What does she dream of, and why do you think she calls it perfect?

Chapter 7

- How does Anna know that the chickens "would not be for eating"?
- Why is Maggie so nice to Sarah, bringing her gifts and offering to teach her to drive a wagon?
- Maggie says, "There are always things to miss. No matter where you are." What do you think she means by this?
- Maggie knows that Sarah "must have a garden" because she loves flowers so much. Is there anything you love so much that you need to have it, wherever you are?

Chapter 8

- When Caleb tells Sarah, "Women don't wear overalls," how does Sarah respond? What do you think this says about her?
- When Sarah runs out into the storm with Jacob, what things do they bring back with them? Why do you think they choose to rescue these things?
- Caleb points out what is missing from Sarah's drawing of the sea. What is it?

Chapter 9

- Why are the children so worried about Sarah going to town alone? What does Anna remember about her mother in this chapter?
- Why is Caleb so relieved when Sarah returns? What does he tell Sarah when she gets back? What do you learn about Caleb's personality in this scene?
- What does Sarah bring with her when she returns? What are the reasons she brings these things?

Plot: What's Happening?

"I will always miss my old home, but the truth of it is I would miss you more."

—Sarah, *Sarah, Plain and Tall*

Sarah, *Plain and Tall* is the story of a loving family that has experienced a great loss. Anna, the narrator, is about twelve years old. Her brother, Caleb, is several years younger. The two children live on the prairie with their father, Jacob, and their two dogs, Nick and Lottie. Anna and Caleb's mother is not present because she died as a result of giving birth to Caleb.

When the book opens, Anna is rolling bread dough while Caleb watches her. It is winter on the prairie and a fire burns in the kitchen. Caleb asks Anna the same questions about his mother over and over again. He was just a day old when his mother died, so Caleb is not able to remember her at all.

Anna, who is old enough to remember her mother, remembers very well how things were after her mom died: "And then the days seemed long and dark like winter days, even though it wasn't winter. And Papa didn't sing."

Although she cares very much for her brother now, Anna tells the reader that she found it hard to love Caleb when he was first born. She says that he was not very pretty, smelled bad, and cried. And the worst thing about Caleb's birth was that her mother passed away the next day.

Jacob, the children's father, returns home from a trip into town. The children welcome him with hugs. Caleb asks his father why he does not sing anymore. Jacob tells him, "I've forgotten the old songs." Jacob then informs the children that he has placed an advertisement in a newspaper for a wife. In the 1800s, women would sometimes answer an ad to be a mother and a wife to a family who did not have one.

Jacob reads the children a letter. The letter is from Sarah Elisabeth Wheaton, a woman from Maine who is answering the ad. She tells the family a little about herself in her first letter. Anna and Caleb think it is important to find out if Sarah sings, like their mother had. Anna tells her father, "Ask her if she sings."

The family all write letters to Sarah in Maine, and she replies to each of them separately. She answers their questions and tells them more about Maine and her life and family there.

Sarah agrees to come and stay with the family for a short time to see if she likes them and if they like her. If they all get along well, Sarah will marry Jacob and stay on the prairie. In Sarah's second letter to Jacob she says, "I will come by train. I will wear a yellow bonnet." And then at the close of her letter she writes, "Tell them I sing."

On the day she arrives, Caleb is very nervous and asks Anna a lot of questions: "Will she be nice?... How far away is Maine?... Will Sarah bring some sea?... Will she like us?" Sarah brings a gray cat named Seal with her, as well as gifts from the sea for Anna and Caleb. The children worry immediately that Sarah will be lonely so far from home. They are concerned that she will miss the ocean, as well as the brother and family she describes in her letters.

Winter turns into spring and Sarah picks flowers for the house. She makes meals for the family, grooms their hair, and, most important, she sings with them. Sarah becomes fond of the animals on the farm where Caleb, Anna, and Jacob live. The family and Sarah exchange stories about the lands they know. Sarah tells Jacob and the children of the ocean and dunes along the coast of Maine: "... there are rock cliffs that rise up at the edge of the sea. And there are hills covered with pine and spruce trees, green with needles." The children tell Sarah about winters on the prairie: "Papa builds a warm fire, and we bake hot biscuits and put on hundreds of sweaters. And if the snow is too high, we stay home from school and make snow people."

Sarah is still with the family when the summer roses start blooming. Matthew and Maggie, neighbors of Anna, Caleb, and Jacob, come to visit and to help Jacob plow a new cornfield. Maggie spends time with Sarah. The two women find that they have things in common and get along well with each other.

Maggie tells Sarah that she too misses the state where she grew up: "I miss the hills of Tennessee sometimes." Sarah confesses to Maggie that she misses her brother, William, and the sea. But Maggie tells Sarah something important: "There are always things to miss. . . . No matter where you are." She helps Sarah understand that there are ways to be more comfortable in a new place, like planting a garden, getting new pets, and learning new skills.

The next morning Sarah tells Jacob that she wants to learn to do the things he does around the farm: ride a horse and drive a wagon. She also wants to travel into town on her own, a wish that makes the children very nervous. Caleb asks Anna, "Why does she want to go to town by herself?. . . To leave us?"

The same morning a terrible rainstorm comes and the family is forced to take shelter in the barn. Sarah runs back out into the bad weather, with Jacob following right after her, to rescue a few important things from the storm. The two return with the chickens Maggie gave to Sarah, the summer roses Jacob had given Sarah, some food, and the seashells Sarah had brought with her from Maine. As they wait for the storm to pass, Caleb notices that the stormy sky is the same colors as the ocean Sarah has described, and that these colors are missing from a drawing she has made.

The day after the storm, Jacob keeps his promise to Sarah. He teaches her how to drive the wagon so that she can go to town by herself. The children watch anxiously. "Why does she have to go away alone?" Caleb wonders. Anna tells him to hush, but then they both escape to the barn where they cry together without Sarah and Jacob seeing them.

The next morning Jacob, Anna, and Caleb watch Sarah climb into the wagon and leave, bound for town. Anna tells the reader, "It was sunny, and I remembered another time when a wagon had taken Mama away. It had been a day just like this day. And Mama had never come back." Papa spends the day quietly working in the fields while the children wait, fretting that she will not return. Just before dark, they finally spot dust rising on the road and Sarah's yellow bonnet comes into sight.

Sarah returns with special gifts, including pencils the color of the sea so that she can finish her drawing. She tells Anna and Caleb that no matter how much she may miss Maine, if she were to leave, she would miss them more. Sarah will stay from now on, and "soon there will be a wedding. Papa says that when the preacher asks if he will have Sarah for his wife, he will answer, 'Ayuh.'"

Thinking about the plot
• Why does Sarah come to stay with this family?
• Why do the children worry that Sarah may leave them?
• What things does Sarah do that make the reader understand she will stay on the prairie?

Setting/Place and Time: Where in the World Are We?

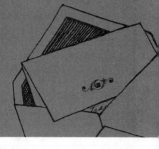

> "There were fields and grass and sky and not much else."
>
> —Anna, *Sarah, Plain and Tall*

Place

The setting of a book is where and when the story takes place. *Sarah, Plain and Tall* takes place in a rural area on the prairie lands of the United States. The prairie is a part of the United States that includes Oklahoma, Kansas, Nebraska, Illinois, South Dakota, and North Dakota. Much of the land there is fairly flat. There are sprawling fields of grass that are perfect for farming corn and wheat. Patricia MacLachlan never tells the reader exactly what state the family lives in, but she provides a vivid picture of the land around the farm and how it changes with each season. She discusses the sky as well as the plants, trees, and animals that inhabit the area.

When telling the reader about winter on the prairie, Anna first describes the sky at that time of year: "Outside the prairie reached out and touched the places where the sky came down." She says that patches of snow and ice cover the landscape and that the days sometimes seem long and dark.

When Sarah asks Caleb and Anna to describe the prairie winters to her, they tell her that it gets very cold there and that they go to school at that time of year. The children wouldn't have gone to school for as many months a year as kids today do. Caleb and Anna would have needed to stay home more often during the other seasons of the year to help out around the farm.

Caleb tells Sarah that it snows a great deal in the winter. The snow gets so deep that they sometimes have to dig their way through it just to feed the farm animals. He says, "When there are bad storms, Papa ties a rope from the house to the barn so no one will get lost." Caleb goes on to tell Sarah that winter winds blow the snow and make the sheep run around.

MacLachlan describes spring on the prairie in great detail. In the spring the land is full of new flowers. The grassy fields bloom with "Indian paintbrush, red and orange, and blue-eyed grass." Sarah arrives in the spring and she and the children pick the paintbrush, as well as clover and prairie violets. Anna notices wild rosebuds that climb up the paddock fence and even describes the Russian olive that her mother had planted.

The animals are out and about around the farm during the spring. The gophers run back and forth across the road. The woodchucks eat quietly in the fields. The cows move toward the cow pond very slowly, "like turtles," as MacLachlan writes. Anna can see marsh hawks fly down behind the barn and hear meadowlarks singing in the distance.

Summertime on the prairie is lovely. The days are longer, it is hot, and the animals still roam the farmland. The sheep are out grazing. The summer winds carry Sarah's songs as she lies in the meadow. The cows move very close to their pond, where there is cool water and trees to shade them from the heat. The dogs, Lottie and Nick, sniff around the children and Sarah. The chickens fuss, leaving tiny footprints in the dirt. Jacob works the horses hard as they plow the fields under the hot summer sun.

The fluffy, featherlike heads of the dandelions blow by in the wind. The summer roses open, and Sarah and the children plant flowers by the porch.

There is another setting that Patricia MacLachlan describes in *Sarah, Plain and Tall*, but it's a place where only one of the characters has ever been. It's the Maine setting that exists in Sarah's memories. The reader can imagine what it is like there based solely on Sarah's descriptions.

Sarah discusses the colors of the ocean: "My favorite colors are the colors of the sea, blue and gray and green, depending on the weather." She also talks about how the water in the ocean is salty and wavy. The ocean stretches out farther than the eye can see. The water gleams "like the sun on glass," Sarah says. Sarah's brother has told her that when he is out on his fishing boat and it is foggy, the water is a color so unique that there is no name for it.

When Sarah first arrives, she brings things from the coast of Maine for the children. She brings Caleb a shell called a moon snail. It is curled and smells like salt from the ocean. Sarah tells Caleb that the seagulls that live on the shore fly up high and carry moon snails in their beaks. The gulls drop the shell so that it crashes on the rocks below. The shell opens. Then the birds swoop down to eat what is inside. For Anna, Sarah brings a sea stone. Sarah tells her that the stone is smooth and round because the water washes over and around it for a long time, wearing away the sharp ridges and edges. These items from Maine, and their descriptions, give the reader a better sense of what Maine looks, smells, and sounds like.

When Sarah's brother goes fishing in Maine, he catches flounder, sea bass, and bluefish. He sees whales in the water and birds flying overhead. Sarah also tells the children about the seals in Maine: "I've touched seals. Real seals. They are cool and slippery and they slide through the water like fish. They can cry and sing. And sometimes they bark, a little like dogs."

The house that Sarah lived in in Maine is tall. The salty air has turned the shingles gray. There are rosebushes near the house and lots of other plants and flowers, too. Sarah describes them: "We have seaside goldenrod and wild asters and woolly ragwort. . . . I had a garden in Maine with dahlias and columbine. And nasturtiums the color of the sun when it sets."

We find out that Sarah's brother, William, has a gray-and-white boat named *Kittiwake*. A kittiwake is a small gull found off the shore of Maine, where William goes to fish. Sarah and William have three aunts who live near them. Sarah says, "They wear silk dresses and no shoes."

Time

Many of the details about *Sarah, Plain and Tall* indicate that it takes place in the late 1800s. In the nineteenth century (1800–1899), the prairie lands of the United States were being settled. People often made their living on farms and did not have any of the modern conveniences we have today.

The family uses a horse-drawn wagon to transport them from place to place. Today, most people travel by car or bus, but this method of travel was not common in the nineteenth century. Anna cooks meals for the family over an open fire. The same fire supplies heat to the house during the cold winter months. This is because there was no electricity back then! Anna would not have had an electric or a gas stove or an oven to cook with, and the house would not have had electric heat. The family lights oil lamps to see in the dark. No electricity meant no electric lights!

Jacob, Anna, and Caleb exchange handwritten letters with Sarah. The story occurs well before e-mail existed. After Sarah arrives, she cuts the family's hair for them rather than bringing them to a barber shop or hair salon, so the reader can guess that such places were not yet common. They all sing together for entertainment rather than watch television or movies, as many people do today.

Another indication that the story takes place in the nineteenth century is that Caleb's mother died giving birth to him at home. Anna tells the reader how she remembers the day her mother died. She says, "They had come for her in a wagon and taken her away to be buried." Medical practices were very different in this time period than they are today. Women who lived in newly settled areas, like the prairie, often gave birth at home because there weren't many doctors' offices nearby. Sometimes there wasn't even a doctor, so a person called a midwife would help a woman have her baby.

Today new medical equipment and well-trained doctors make childbirth much safer. In the nineteenth century these things were not available, so if a problem occurred, the mother or baby often died.

MacLachlan further establishes the nineteenth-century rural setting by describing the daily activities of the family. Most of what they do involves maintaining the farm. Jacob plows the fields with a horse-drawn plow. He does this so that he can plant a crop that he can harvest later. The children care for the animals and the house. Anna tells the reader, "Caleb and I did our chores. . . . We shoveled out the stalls and laid down new hay. We fed the sheep. We swept and straightened and carried wood and water." Anna is also responsible for making the family's meals. She cooks stews and breads for her brother and father.

Thinking about the setting

- Where does *Sarah, Plain and Tall* take place? How does the author tell the reader this?
- What is the second setting of the book? In what ways does the reader find out what this place is like?
- When does *Sarah, Plain and Tall* take place? How does the author let the reader know this?
- What is your home like? How does it compare with Caleb and Anna's home on the prairie?

Themes/Layers of Meaning: Is That What It *Really* Means?

"Soon there will be a wedding....
There will be Sarah's sea, blue and
gray and green, hanging on the wall.
And songs, old ones and new."

—Anna, *Sarah, Plain and Tall*

The theme of a book is the subject matter about which the author is writing. Themes are the main ideas on which the book is based. *Sarah, Plain and Tall* has several themes. Let's investigate them!

New beginnings

The quotation above, spoken by Anna at the end of *Sarah, Plain and Tall*, illustrates one of the novel's main themes: new beginnings. Anna's words speak of the future of the family. She is hopeful about the new things that have happened to her recently. She looks forward to even more new things to come now that Sarah is staying. At the same time, she acknowledges the importance of keeping memories of her mother close to her heart.

When the novel opens, Anna is patiently retelling Caleb stories of their mother, whose passing has left an emptiness in their lives.

They all feel alone without her but show this in different ways. Caleb never knew his mother because the day after he was born she died from complications from the birth. He has Anna tell him about their mother so that he can try to imagine what it would have been like to have her in his life.

Anna thinks about her mother all the time. She recalls the songs they used to sing together. She remembers the last thing her mother said to her before she died, "Isn't he beautiful, Anna?"

It is obvious that Jacob misses his wife. When Caleb asked his father why he doesn't sing anymore, Jacob tells him that he has forgotten the old songs. What he means is that he has been too sad to sing without his wife. He sees the chance to bring a new wife and mother to their home as "a way to remember" the old songs. When Jacob places the advertisement that Sarah answers, he is making a big step toward a new beginning for his family. It has been many years since his wife's death, and he wants to bring happiness into their lives. Caleb and Anna will have a mother figure and Jacob will have companionship.

When Sarah arrives at the farm, she breathes new life into the sad family. Sarah brings stories of a faraway place called Maine. She has a nurturing personality. Sarah shows the family that she's loving, caring, and gentle. Anna says, "Sarah brushed my hair and tied it up in back with a rose velvet ribbon she had brought from Maine." Then later, she says, "Sarah kissed us all, even my father, who looked surprised."

Most important, Sarah brings a desire to have a new beginning of her own. For Sarah, moving to the prairie will allow her to feel needed by a family again, since her brother has a wife to care for him now. "I miss my brother William. But he is married. The house is hers now. Not mine any longer," Sarah says. It also means that she will get to experience a brand-new place to live that is very different from the one she grew up in.

With Anna's closing words of hope, "Soon there will be a wedding. . . . There will be Sarah's sea, blue and gray and green, hanging on the wall. And songs, old ones and new," the author conveys a deep message. Sarah herself is a new beginning for a family that will always miss and love their mother and wife, but who desperately need light in their lives again. At the same time, this family is a chance for Sarah to make a new start, too.

MacLachlan makes it clear that although the children love and welcome Sarah into their lives, this in no way lessens the love that they have for their deceased mother. They still miss her because there are always things to miss, even when your life has become happy again. The case is the same with Sarah and her brother, William. Although she misses him and loves him dearly, she has started a new chapter in her life and loves Jacob and the children, too. But loving them does not make her love or miss William any less.

Family

Another central theme in *Sarah, Plain and Tall* is that of family. Patricia MacLachlan once said, "I see that I write books about brothers and sisters, about what makes up a family, what works and what is nurturing."

In this novel, the author has created a special and unique family. Today, most families are not formed by placing advertisements, like Jacob does. They are a loving family, nonetheless. Sarah is not the biological mother of Anna and Caleb, and she did not know or love Jacob before she came to stay on the prairie. But, by the close of the novel, Sarah interacts with the children and Jacob just as a mother or wife would. Anna tells the reader, "We eat our night meal by candlelight, the four of us. Sarah has brought candles from town. And nasturtium seeds for her garden, and a book of songs to teach us. It is late, and Caleb is nearly sleeping by his plate and Sarah is smiling at my father." Many people think that a family is made up of a mom and a dad and their children. But, in reality, families are made up of all kinds of people, with all different kinds of relationships with one another. MacLachlan shows the reader that these families are as good as any other.

MacLachlan reinforces family as an important theme in *Sarah, Plain and Tall* by showing the loving relationship that Caleb, Anna, and Jacob have with one another, even before Sarah's arrival. Anna and Caleb have a sweet, close sibling relationship. Anna teases Caleb by telling him that he looked like a ball of bread dough when he was born because he had no hair. This makes Caleb smile. MacLachlan shows their special brother-sister bond when the two go into the barn together to cry. They worry about Sarah wanting to go into town alone, so they comfort each other.

The reader also sees the closeness of Jacob and his children:

> Papa put his arms around me and put his nose in my hair.
>
> "Nice soapy smell, that stew," he said.
>
> I laughed. "That's my hair."
>
> Caleb came over and threw his arms around Papa's neck and hung down as Papa swung him back and forth, and the dogs sat up.

Abandonment

One more important theme in *Sarah, Plain and Tall* is a less positive, but equally important one: abandonment. In this story, Jacob, Anna, and especially Caleb feel abandoned by their wife and mother. We see this theme expressed most vividly through Caleb.

Caleb's mother died just after giving birth to him, so he never had a mother figure in his life. When Jacob tells the children about Sarah, Caleb worries before he even meets her. He asks Anna, "Do you think she'll come? And will she stay? What if she thinks we are loud and pesky?... What if she comes and doesn't like our house?"

As Anna and Caleb await Sarah's arrival, Caleb asks Anna, "Is my face clean?... Can my face be *too* clean?... Will she like us?" After Sarah comes to the prairie, Caleb still worries. When Sarah expresses her desire to go to town alone for a day, Caleb gets very upset. He asks Anna, "Why?...Why does she have to go away alone?" After Sarah goes to town and returns to them, Caleb bursts into tears. "Seal was very worried!" he cries to Sarah. Sarah puts her arms around Caleb, and he continues to cry, "And the house is too small, we thought! And I am loud and pesky!" Sarah has not abandoned him. Caleb feels so relieved that Sarah has returned that he finally confesses his fears to her.

MacLachlan explores this sad theme with gentle humor, showing the reader that even though bad things sometimes happen in life, good things can come from them. In this book, even though Caleb's biological mother died, Sarah has come into his life and brought new happiness to it.

Thinking about themes
• What do you think is the most important theme in *Sarah, Plain and Tall*?
• What are some different kinds of families that you know?
• Have you ever had a new beginning in your life? What was it? How did it change things for you?

The way an author develops the people in a story is called characterization. The writer helps the reader understand the people in the book by describing what they look like, how they act, the things they say and do, how they interact with the other characters, and how they react to different situations. This is a list of the characters in *Sarah, Plain and Tall*, followed by descriptions of the most important ones.

Anna	a young girl, the narrator of the story
Caleb	Anna's younger brother
Jacob	Anna and Caleb's father
Sarah Wheaton	a woman from Maine who answers an ad to be a wife and mother
Maggie	a neighbor of Jacob's family who befriends Sarah
Matthew	Maggie's husband, a friend of Jacob's
Rose	a young daughter of Maggie and Matthew
Violet	a young daughter of Maggie and Matthew

Anna: Anna is the narrator of *Sarah, Plain and Tall*, which means she is the person speaking to the reader, telling the story of her family. She is a young girl, and although the author never says exactly how old she is, the reader can guess that she may be about twelve or thirteen years old. Anna is old enough to do many of the household chores, like cooking, but she is still young enough to want a mother figure in her life to guide her.

It's clear from the beginning of the book that Anna misses her mother deeply. She says to one of the dogs, "I miss Mama." She talks about how her mother's death has stayed with her, even though it was many years ago: "I looked at the long dirt road that crawled across the plains, remembering the morning that Mama had died, cruel and sunny. They had come for her in a wagon and taken her away to be buried. And then the cousins and aunts and uncles had come and tried to fill up the house. But they couldn't."

Caleb's birth caused Anna's mother to die. This made it hard for Anna to accept Caleb. Anna loves Caleb very much now, but admits to the reader that it was hard to love him when he was first born. She says, "It took three whole days for me to love him. . . ."

Anna has, in many ways, taken over the role her mother would have filled. She is very responsible, especially for such a young girl. Anna also does many of the chores around the farm, like feeding the animals. She prepares meals for the family and watches over Caleb. When Jacob reads Sarah's letter to Anna and Caleb, the first thing Anna does is look at Caleb. She has become like a mother to Caleb, so she wants to make sure he is not upset by what the letter says. Anna sees that the letter has made Caleb smile, so she knows he is all right.

Although she has had to grow up in many ways since her mother's death, Anna welcomes the presence of a mother figure in her life to make her feel like a girl again. Anna tells the reader, "Sarah brushed my hair and tied it up in back with a rose velvet ribbon she had brought from Maine. She brushed hers long and free and tied it back, too, and we stood side by side looking into the mirror. I looked taller, like Sarah, and fair and thin. And with my hair pulled back I looked a little like her daughter. Sarah's daughter."

Caleb: Caleb is Anna's younger brother, who is probably about seven or eight years old. Caleb and Anna's mother died the day after she gave birth to him. He never got a chance to know his mother because he was only a day old when she passed away.

Caleb worries constantly that he will be left again, as he was when his mother died. This makes him very vulnerable. The way Caleb relates to Sarah illustrates this characteristic of his personality. He tracks Sarah's every movement, trying to guess if she is happy enough to stay. Anna tells the reader, "Papa was quiet and shy with Sarah, and so was I. But Caleb talked to Sarah from morning until the light left the sky.

"'Where are you going?' he asked. 'To do what?'" Caleb also hangs on to the little clues in Sarah's comments. "Sarah said winter. That means Sarah will stay," he reports to Anna. Caleb's fears also make him cry frequently. He depends on his older sister for comfort when his feelings overwhelm him. He frequently leans up against her or grabs her hand when he feels afraid. Anna tells the reader that when Sarah arrives she brings a conch shell from Maine as a gift: "She put it to Caleb's ear, then mine. Papa listened, too. Then Sarah listened once more, with a look so sad and far away that Caleb leaned against me."

Caleb takes pleasure in the smallest things he learns from Sarah. He says cute, funny things and is playful because he is so young. The author makes it obvious that he enjoys having a woman to act as a mother in his life. When she explains to him that there is a flower called woolly ragwort in Maine, he laughs at its name and makes up a song about the plant. When Sarah teaches him that *ayuh* means "yes" in Maine, he repeatedly uses the term, even after the conversation has turned to another subject, "Do you want more stew?" Sarah asks Caleb. He replies with an "ayuh."

It's also clear how much Caleb likes learning new things from Sarah when she teaches the children to swim. MacLachlan tells us: "Caleb lay on his back and learned how to blow streams of water high in the air like a whale," while Anna "sank like a bucket filled with water." Sarah explains to Caleb what the waves in the ocean are like: "'Like this?' asked Caleb, and he pushed a wave at Sarah, making her cough and laugh."

Caleb also takes pleasure from teaching Sarah things about the prairie. When he tells her about the winter winds, "Caleb stood up and ran like the wind, and the sheep ran after him. Sarah and I watched him jump over rock and gullies, the sheep behind him, stiff legged and fast. He circled the field, the sun making the top of his hair golden."

Jacob: Jacob is the father of Anna and Caleb. He has a home and farm for his family on the prairie. He works the land himself, with the help of Caleb's small hands and occasionally the more capable hands of his neighbor, Matthew. He also maintains the house and cares for the animals on the farm, so the reader knows he is a very hard worker.

One of the most important things about Jacob is that he is a caring person. This is very obvious in his relationship with his children. The reader learns that when they've had snow in the winter months, he takes his children to school in the wagon and bakes them warm bread. After Jacob receives a letter from Sarah expressing that she'd like to come to the prairie to see what she thinks of their family, Jacob informs Anna and Caleb, "Sarah has said she will come for a month's time if we wish her to. . . . To see how it is. Just to see." He asks his children for their approval because their happiness is even more important than his own. Caleb says, "I think . . . I think that it would be good—to say yes." Then Jacob looks to Anna for her response: "I say yes," she replies. It is only when he has the approval of both that Jacob is able to say for sure that he will accept Sarah's offer.

The day Jacob goes to pick up Sarah at the train station, he makes the extra effort to look nice and make a good impression on her. Anna says, "Papa got up early for the long day's trip to the train and back. He brushed his hair so slick and shiny that Caleb laughed. He wore a clean blue shirt, and a belt instead of suspenders." After Sarah arrives, Jacob wants to make her happy and comfortable in her new surroundings. He re-creates a dune for her in the barn, which is something she misses from Maine:

"Next to the barn was Papa's mound of hay for bedding, nearly half as tall as the barn, covered with canvas to keep the rain from rotting it. Papa carried the wooden ladder from the barn and leaned it up against the hay.

"'There.' He smiled at Sarah. 'Our dune.'"

MacLachlan makes it clear that Jacob is happy to have Sarah in his life. He teaches her to drive the wagon and to plow, he accepts her help fixing the roof, and he lets her cut his hair. He understands that Sarah is independent and lets her be herself. When Sarah explains to Jacob that she wants to be able to go into town alone, he says, "That's a fair thing, Sarah." When the children are upset waiting to see if Sarah will return from her trip to town, Jacob explains, "Sarah is Sarah. She does things her own way, you know." From this, the reader can tell Jacob respects Sarah's individuality.

Jacob's caring nature is also displayed in the thoughtful gestures he makes toward Sarah: "And then Papa came, just before the rain, bringing Sarah the first roses of summer." The reader also sees that Jacob is sensitive and kind when, during the big storm, he follows Sarah back out into the rain and wind to help her save the chickens she loves.

Sarah Wheaton: Sarah is a woman from Maine who responds to an advertisement she reads in the newspaper. The advertisement was for a woman to be a companion to Jacob and to act as a mother to Anna and Caleb.

Sarah is the focus of *Sarah, Plain and Tall*, so the reader learns a great deal about her. At the beginning, the reader finds out about Sarah from the letters she writes to Anna, Caleb, and Jacob. In her first letter to Jacob, Sarah is very straightforward. She does not hesitate to tell him things about herself that he may not like. She writes, "I am strong and I work hard and I am willing to travel. But I am not mild mannered."

Sarah displays that she is not mild mannered in person after she arrives on the prairie. When Caleb tells her that women don't wear overalls, Sarah simply says, "This woman does." It is through direct, blunt statements that Sarah shows her independence. She wants to be able to do things on her own. Sarah insists that Jacob teach her things: "I want to learn how to ride a horse. And then I want to learn how to drive the wagon."

We also learn that Sarah can be stubborn when she has her mind set on something. When Sarah tells Jacob that she wants to learn to ride Jacob's horse, Jacob says no: "Not Jack. Jack is sly." Sarah responds, "I am sly, too." Her persistence makes Jacob smile, but still he says, "Ayuh [yes]. But not Jack." Sarah raises her voice to make Jacob understand that she is serious: "Yes, Jack!"

Sarah is the type of woman who does not like to be told what she can and can't do, or what she is or is not capable of doing. She is willful and determined. Jacob tells her that he has to fix the roof right away before a bad storm comes. "*We* will fix the roof," Sarah tells him. And then she adds, "I've done it before. I know about roofs. I am a good carpenter." And so Jacob and Sarah climb the ladder to the roof to repair it together. Anna notices that Sarah is wearing overalls like her papa's: "Overalls that *were* Papa's."

Sarah is a free spirit. She does things that make her happy, even if other people might think her actions are unusual or silly. This is shown when she decides to teach the children to swim in the cow pond, a possibility the children had never considered before.

There is also a soft, gentle side to Sarah's personality. She likes to pick wildflowers to dry and hang up. She likes to brush Anna's hair and pull it back with pretty ribbon.

Sarah loves animals. She brings her gray cat, Seal, with her from Maine. She adores the dogs that live on the farm. Sarah befriends the chickens Maggie gives her. "Sarah loved the chickens. She clucked back to them and fed them grain. They followed her, shuffling and scratching primly in the dirt. I knew they would not be for eating," Anna tells us. Sarah even runs back out into a terrible rainstorm to save them.

Sarah also loves the sheep that inhabit the farm. Anna says, "The sheep made Sarah smile. She sank her fingers into their thick, coarse wool. She talked to them, running with the lambs, letting them suck on her fingers." When a lamb dies, the reader also sees that Sarah is protective of the children. Sarah does not allow Anna or Caleb near the dead animal, and she sits on the porch alone after Jacob buries it.

The gentle side of Sarah's personality is also shown in the way that she misses her home and her brother and aunts she left in

Maine. When the neighbors, Maggie and Matthew, come to visit for the day, Maggie and Sarah discuss Sarah's homesickness. "You are lonely, yes?" Maggie asks Sarah. This makes Sarah's eyes fill with tears, and she confesses, "I miss the sea." Anna overhears as Sarah goes on to tell Maggie, "I miss my brother William. . . . There are three old aunts who all squawk together like crows at dawn. I miss them, too."

Thinking about the characters

- Is there a character in *Sarah, Plain and Tall* you think is a little like you? How so? If not, do any of the characters seem like someone else in your life? in what ways?
- Which of the characters do you like the most? the least? Why?
- Are Anna and Caleb similar to kids you know who are the same age? How are they different?

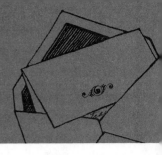

Award winner

The most overwhelming opinion of *Sarah, Plain and Tall* is that it is award-worthy. *Sarah, Plain and Tall* won the 1985 Scott O'Dell Award for Historical Fiction for Children, which is awarded to a commendable book published for children or young adults. The book also won the 1986 Christopher Award, which is "presented to the producers, directors, and writers of books, motion pictures, and television specials that affirm the highest values of the human spirit." And Patricia MacLachlan's novel was awarded the prestigious John Newbery Medal from the American Library Association in 1986. These are only a few of the many awards and honors that Patricia MacLachlan's wonderful story has earned.

Before winning so many awards, the book received a lot of praise from book reviewers and librarians. One reviewer from *School Library Journal* called it "a book that is filled with wisdom, gentle humor, and the practical concerns necessary for a satisfying life." This means that Patricia MacLachlan has created a story with characters who are sensible and funny, and who care for and worry about one another.

The reviewer went on to say, "Through a simple sentence or phrase, aspects of each character's personality—strength, stubbornness, a sense of humor—are brought to light. Refreshingly, this novel portrays children as receptive to the love, nurturing, and attention that a stepparent can offer—and the willingness to return the affection." The reviewer admired MacLachlan's ability to describe her characters fully with only a few carefully chosen words. The way Caleb and Anna readily accept the love of a stepparent is noteworthy. Blended families were not as common in the past as they are today, and people were less accepting of them. Loving your family, regardless of the way it's made up, is important and MacLachlan has captured that in this book.

A different reviewer said that *Sarah, Plain and Tall* is "the simplest of love stories expressed in the simplest of prose. Embedded in these unadorned [simple] declarative sentences about ordinary people, actions, animals, facts, objects, and colors are evocations [suggestions] of the deepest feelings of loss and fear, love and hope." MacLachlan's characters are ordinary people who live simple lives. But she expresses very deep emotions through them. Anna, Caleb, and Jacob have experienced a great loss, and it has affected each of them. But they continue to love one another and enjoy life. The author uses simple sentence structure and vocabulary to show this. She does not let the important ideas of love and family get bogged down by including too many details or challenging words.

Historical fiction

Not every reviewer loved *Sarah, Plain and Tall*. One criticism of the novel is that it may not be historically accurate. It is a historical fiction book, which means that Patricia MacLachlan made up a story based on things that really did happen or did exist in history. For instance, you read in the "How *Sarah, Plain and Tall* Came About" section that a woman named Sarah really did exist. She was actually a relative of Patricia MacLachlan and she answered an advertisement to be a wife and mother to a family. The time period and setting of the book also existed in real life. The author has set her book in the 1800s in the American Midwest and has written about things going on in that time period just as they were in reality.

But did she? One critic has said that the only problem with the book is that the time period is not as historically accurate as it could be: "The realities of nineteenth-century social mores [standards] are at odds with the practicality of all of this. It was unusual (although not impossible) for a woman to travel such distances alone, and much more than unusual for her to stay with a man not related to her without another woman in the house. Had she done so, however, it is unlikely that she could return home afterward with her reputation intact... the story as told is highly uncharacteristic of its time and place."

This reviewer thinks it is unlikely that a woman would have traveled alone all the way from Maine to the prairie to stay with a man she does not know. This makes the story seem more made-up than real. The reviewer goes on to say that the characters don't seem to be doing as much work as they would have needed to do to maintain the farm. Sarah and the children have time to lie in the fields, pick flowers, or go swimming. The reviewer tells us that, in reality, the number of hours of hard work it took to keep the farm going would not have allowed them the time to do these things.

The reviewer also says that it was also not strictly historically accurate for Sarah to have been doing "man's work" and for Papa to have been doing "woman's work." During that time period, people filled traditional male or female roles, even on the farm. Jacob would have cared for the land and the house, while Sarah would have taken care of the people inside the house. Jacob would have done the plowing and roof-fixing. Sarah would have kept the family fed and cared for the children and animals. The two adults would not have done jobs traditionally done by the other very often. The reviewer says: "While none of this was impossible, neither was it typical. Division of labor on a farm was a matter of practicality as well as custom. Papa would not often have been in the house enough to tend bread, and Sarah would have plenty to do without taking up plowing." The fact that the author has them doing just that throughout the book makes the story less believable for this reviewer.

Although this reviewer found fault with *Sarah, Plain and Tall,* most reviewers argue that the book is perfect. A reviewer from the *New York Times* newspaper wrote that "this gentle book cannot fail to touch readers." Award committees, parents, teachers, and kids all seem to agree.

Thinking about what others think about
Sarah, Plain and Tall

- Do you think that Patricia MacLachlan's book should have won lots of awards? Are there other award-winning books you have read that were better or worse? How so?

- Two reviewers said that Patricia MacLachlan uses simple sentences and only a few details to tell the reader a lot about the characters and their feelings. Can you find an example of a sentence or paragraph like this?

- What do you think about the fact that a reviewer said that the book is not completely historically accurate at times? Do you think this changes the importance of the book's messages?

Glossary

bonnet a baby's or woman's hat, tied with strings under the chin

buzzard a large bird of prey, similar to a vulture, with a hooked beak and long, sharp claws

clatter to bang together noisily

collapse to fall down suddenly from weakness

conch the spiral-shaped shell of a marine animal

dune a sand hill made by the wind near the ocean or a large lake or in a desert

dusk the time of day after sunset when it is nearly dark

eerie strange and frightening

feisty lively or frisky

fetch to go after and bring back something or somebody

flax a plant with blue flowers and long leaves that produces oil and fiber

gleams shines

gully a long, narrow ravine or ditch

hearthstone stone flooring laid in front of a fireplace

hitch to join something to a vehicle

killdeer a type of bird with a black chest

mica any type of clear or colored minerals that have crystallized and can separate easily into very thin layers

paddock an enclosed field or area where horses can graze or exercise

pesky troublesome

plow (plough) to turn over soil using a piece of farm equipment pulled by an animal or a tractor

primly in a formal and proper way

pungent when something has a strong taste or smell

rascal a mischievous person or animal

reins straps attached to a bridle to control or guide a horse

roamer a person or animal that wanders around with no particular destination or purpose

scuttling a quick shuffling pace

shingles thin, flat pieces of wood or other material used to cover outside walls or roofs

sly crafty, cunning, secretive

sputter to make popping, spitting, or coughing noises

squall a sudden, violent wind that usually brings rain, snow, or sleet with it

squint to nearly close one's eyes in order to see better

tumbleweed a bushy plant in western North America that dries up in the fall, breaks off from its roots, and blows around in the wind

whicker a horse's whinny or neigh

windbreak a shelter from the wind

wretched miserable or unfortunate

"I think I am a writer because I wanted to put thoughts on paper and have someone read them. It is that simple."

—Patricia MacLachlan

Patricia MacLachlan says that she can sense when she is entering a writing phase: "I can always tell when I'm about to start writing. I go through cycles in reading. When I'm beginning to start to write something, I start reading what I think of as good literature. I read things with wonderful language." She also listens to what she thinks of as good music when she's preparing to write something new. "Then all of a sudden I wake up in the morning one day and I go to the typewriter and I'm ready to write," MacLachlan says. She credits great children's books, as well as great adult books, as sources of motivation: "My inspiration for writing is all the wonderful books that I read as a child and that I still read. I think that for those of us who write, when we find a wonderful book written by someone else, we don't really get jealous, we get inspired, and that's kind of the mark of what a good writer is."

When asked if she researches the books she writes, she said, "I don't think I do any formal research. Life is my research." When she finally is at the point where she is ready to sit down at the typewriter, MacLachlan says, "I always begin with a character. I write a chapter about the character and what he or she is doing, thinking, but I don't know what the story is about yet." MacLachlan also says, "Plot was always my downfall until I learned that basically character and plot amount to the same thing. One grows from the other. As I get to know my characters they let me know what they need. . . . It's a fluid, organic [natural], and even a little mysterious process." By letting her characters speak to her, the author lets the story unfold on its own: "I never work from an outline, and often I don't know how the story will end."

When she creates her characters and stories, Patricia MacLachlan thinks it is important to show sadness and happiness at the same time. She depicts these emotions within the same character because that is how people are in real life, and life is what inspires her. MacLachlan says, "I think life is a mixture of humor and sadness and poignancy and grief, all these things mixed in together. I think that books in a sense maybe don't change lives, but they have a great impact on children's lives. There's a good deal in this world that is not happy and yet there are moments here or there that I try to illuminate, the kind of thoughtful, pensive moments."

When asked about the time of day and spaces she finds best for writing, MacLachlan says, "My best time of day as a writer . . . is between five-thirty and eight in the morning, when I make what at the time seem to me to be the most startling observations. The observations, mind you, that later as I write them become as common as the odd glass of water, the coffee dregs, the garbage of the day—these things, surprise or no surprise, are what life and literature are made of." She also says that she can pretty much write in any space, even "when everyone is bumping around the house talking or asking me questions because it just seems like a normal kind of thing." As long as she has a typewriter and a window nearby, she is able to write. MacLachlan writes about the ordinary, but amazing, things she finds in everyday life, so she does not need to escape to create beautiful literature. She can write with her family around her, living life and carrying on as they normally would.

Patricia MacLachlan's main motivation for writing children's books is "to show children that I value them and that they are important, and what they say is important, and that they can change lives, and that acts have consequences, and things they do have consequences. So I want them to see themselves as valued in books."

For aspiring writers

Patricia MacLachlan says that the most important thing a person needs in order to be a children's book writer is a love of children's books. This may seem obvious, but she has deeper reasons for believing this. MacLachlan says, "Writing for children is special because I think children read with a great true belief in what they're reading." MacLachlan also emphasizes that writers should read as much as they can: "One must understand the far reaches of children's books because they're really about many of the same subjects as adults are concerned with." She has said that truly good books appeal to people of all ages: "Good books have things for children, things for adolescents, and things for adults in them. They're many-leveled, and I like that part of them."

For kids who are aspiring writers, MacLachlan has these wise words to share: "I feel it's crucial that kids who aspire to write understand that I have to rewrite and revise as much as they do. Ours is such a perfectionist society—I see too many kids who believe that if they can't get it right the first time, they aren't writers."

- **Start with a character:** Patricia MacLachlan always starts her book with a character in mind and then develops the story around that character or characters. Think of a person, real or imaginary, and write down important things about him or her, such as, what does this person look like? Where does she live? Where does he or she go? What does he do? Whom does she talk to? What does he see? How does she feel? Create a short story based on your idea of a really interesting character.

- **Put it in a letter:** Just as Sarah exchanged letters with Jacob, Anna, and Caleb, find a pen pal and write to him or her. A pen pal is a buddy with whom you write back and forth, telling them about your life, where you live, your family, whatever is happening to you that you want to share. You can do this over e-mail or the "snail mail" way by sending a letter through the mail like they did in the nineteenth century. Make sure you check with an adult before corresponding over the Internet. Check out Kids' Space Connection at www.ks_connection.org for international pen pals.

- **Wanted:** Jacob places an advertisement in order to find women who might be interested in being a mother and wife. Write an advertisement for a person or thing you might like to have in your life. It could be a new friend, a parent, or even a new pet.

Make sure to include the important characteristics you would like in that person: This can include anything from being able to dance to being able to fetch a newspaper. It can also include qualities like being kind, smart, or funny.

• **Add a scene:** Think of an event that took place in *Sarah, Plain and Tall* that the author did not tell you much about. Maybe it's what happened when Jacob picked up Sarah at the train station. Or perhaps it is what Sarah did while she was in town by herself. Write the scene to fill in the blank for yourself!

• **A wedding journal:** At the end of *Sarah, Plain and Tall* Anna tells the reader, "Soon there will be a wedding." Who would attend the wedding? What would the ceremony be like? What would they eat? Where would they have the wedding? Pretend that you are Sarah or Jacob keeping a diary of the special event.

Activities

• **Plant a garden:** Sarah and her family find many different kinds of flowers on the prairie. Make a list of all the prairie flowers mentioned in the book and the ones Sarah says grow in Maine, and do some research about them. Find out what type of soil they thrive in, how much water and light they need, and then plant seeds in a place where they can grow well.

• **Sing!:** Singing is important to Jacob, Anna, and Caleb because it makes them feel happy and reminds them of their wife and mother. Sarah sings with them, and Caleb makes up a song about the woolly ragwort for her. Make up songs of your own about things and people in your life. Think of nice lyrics and a melody. Make your songs funny or silly, happy or sad. Sing about nature, as Caleb does, or sing about things like school, or soccer practice, or your brother's smelly feet!

• **See the sea:** Sarah describes the ocean in detail throughout *Sarah, Plain and Tall*. Think about her descriptions of the sea, and create a picture of it in your mind. Then, make a real picture of it! Using colored pencils, crayons, or watercolor paints, draw or paint a seascape. You may have visited the beach yourself, or you may even live near one. Go ahead and include any details you want based on your own experiences with the ocean, too.

- **Pick a bouquet:** Sarah loves all kinds of flowers. She picks wildflowers and even keeps a garden. Spend an hour outside on a nice day picking flowers near your home or school. (Be sure to get permission before picking flowers on property that doesn't belong to you.) Then, hang them upside-down somewhere to dry. Once they've dried completely, you'll be able to enjoy their beauty for a long time.

- **Locate it:** Where in the world is Maine? And where is the prairie? Find a detailed map of the entire United States. Locate these places on the map. How far away from each other are they? How long do you think it would take to travel from one place to the other back in the 1800s? How long do you think it would take now?

- **Take a dip:** Sarah speaks about her love of the ocean, and part of that love was swimming in its salty waves. She teaches the children to swim in the cow pond. Whatever body of water is near you, whether it be an ocean, a lake, or pool, go for a swim. It's fun and great exercise. Never go swimming unattended, though, or in an area with big waves or fast-moving currents. If you don't know how to swim, learn! Ask your parents or older sibling to teach you, if they know how, or take lessons at a local pool or YMCA. You'll be happy you took the plunge!

- **Cover to cover:** The cover of *Sarah, Plain and Tall* shows Sarah sitting with Caleb and Anna on the porch of the house while Sarah cuts Caleb's hair. The front cover of a book is important because it is what makes a first impression on the reader. It should reflect something meaningful or important about the book. If you were given the job of designing the book's cover, what picture would you use? Draw a new cover for *Sarah, Plain and Tall*, using images from the book that mean the most to you.

• **See it on the big screen:** There are three movies that were made based on the characters from *Sarah, Plain and Tall*: *Sarah, Plain and Tall*; *Skylark*; and *Winter's End*. Have an adult rent the videos or DVDs, and watch them after you have read the books in the series. Compare and contrast the books with their movie versions. How do they differ? Do you like one version better than the other? Do the actors in the films look like what you imagined the characters in the books to look like? Do the farm and house look like what you imagined?

• **Bake bread:** Just like Sarah, Anna, and Jacob do, you can make a warm, delicious loaf of fresh bread to have at your next meal. Have an adult help you when using the oven.

Ingredients
¾ cup rolled (old-fashioned) oats
1¼ cup warm water
4 tablespoons oil or melted butter
4 tablespoons honey
2 cups whole wheat flour (white flour was available but costly at the time) + 2–4 extra cups as needed
2 teaspoons baking powder
¼ teaspoon baking soda
½ teaspoon salt

Directions

1. Combine oats, water, oil or butter, and honey in a small bowl. Let the mixture sit for about five minutes so the oats soften.

2. In a separate, large bowl, combine 2 cups of the flour with the baking powder, baking soda, and salt. Stir until the ingredients are combined.

3. Add the wet ingredients to the dry ingredients and combine.

4. Add more flour, 1 cup at a time, and mix until the ingredients come together and start pulling away from the sides of the bowl. The dough will feel thick, elastic, and a little sticky.

5. Put ½ cup of flour on your work surface. Knead the dough by pressing and turning it over and over 20–30 times.

6. Spread a small amount of oil on the inside of a clean bowl. Place the kneaded dough into the bowl and let it sit for 30 minutes.

7. Preheat oven to 350 degrees.

8. Form dough into a round loaf and bake on a greased cookie sheet for 45 minutes, or until a toothpick poked in the center comes out dry.

9. Eat warm with butter or honey.

• **She sells seashells:** Sarah fondly remembers the seashells in Maine. The next time you are at the ocean, go shell hunting! Collect different types of shells in a bucket. Rinse the sand off them, and try to identify what type of shells they are. A field guidebook such as *National Audubon Society First Field Guide: Shells* will help you do this. Use the shells to decorate your bedroom, or save them in a special place to remind you of the beach.

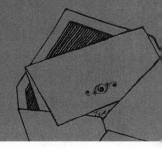

Related Reading

**Other books in the *Sarah, Plain and Tall* series
by Patricia MacLachlan**

Skylark (1994)

Caleb's Story (2001)

Other books by Patricia MacLachlan

All the Places to Love (1994)

Arthur, for the Very First Time (1980)

Baby (1993)

Cassie Binegar (1982)

The Facts and Fictions of Minna Pratt (1988)

It's Fine to Be Nine (2000)

It's Heaven to Be Seven (2000)

Journey (1993)

Mama One, Mama Two (1982)

Moon Stars, Frogs, and Friends (1980)

Painting the Wind (2003)

Seven Kisses in a Row (1983)

The Sick Day (1979)

Three Names (1994)

Through Grandpa's Eyes (1980)

Tomorrow's Wizard (1982)

Unclaimed Treasures (1984)

What You Know First (1995)

Movies based on Patricia MacLachlan's books

Sarah, Plain and Tall, 1991 (DVD and VHS)

Skylark, 1993 (DVD and VHS)

Winter's End, 1999 (DVD and VHS)

Books about the prairie—fiction

Across the Wide and Lonesome Prairie: The Oregon Trail Diary of Hattie Campbell, 1847 (Dear America) by Kristiana Gregory

Caddie Woodlawn by Carol Ryrie Brink

Little House on the Prairie by Laura Ingalls Wilder

Little Town on the Prairie by Laura Ingalls Wilder

My Face to the Wind: The Diary of Sarah Jane Price, a Prairie Teacher, 1881 (Dear America) by Jim Murphy

Prairie Songs by Pam Conrad

Books about the prairie—nonfiction

If You're Not from the Prairie by Dave Bouchard

A Prairie Alphabet by Jo Bannatyne-Cugnet and Yvette Moore

Books about abandonment—fiction

Homecoming by Cynthia Voigt

The Road to Home by Jane Auch

Books about unusual family situations—fiction

Agony of Alice by Phyllis Reynolds Naylor

The Great Gilly Hopkins by Katherine Paterson

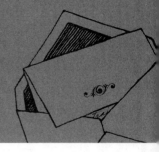

Bibliography

Books

MacLachlan, Patricia. *Sarah, Plain and Tall.* New York: Harper Collins, 1985.

Periodicals

Horn Book Magazine. November/December 1989, "Dialogue Between Charlotte Zolotow and Patricia MacLachlan," pp. 736–745.

Jones, Trev. *School Library Journal.* "A Review of *Sarah, Plain and Tall*," May 1985, vol. 31: pp. 92–93.

McMahon, Thomas, ed. *Authors & Artists for Young Adults.* Volume 18, 1996, pp. 169–177.

Saxton, Martha. *The New York Times Book Review.* May 19, 1985, Late City Final Edition, Section 7, p. 20,

Senick, Gerard J., ed. *Children's Literature Review.* Volume 14, 1998, pp. 177–186.

Trosky, Susan M., ed. *Contemporary Authors.* Volume 136, 1992, pp. 261–263.

Web sites

Educational Paperback Association:
www.edupaperback.org/authorbios/MacLachlan_Patricia.html

Horn Book Magazine online:

www.hbook.com/exhibit/article_macleod.html

Teachers @ Random:

www.randomhouse.com/teachers/authors/macl.html